The VITAL Connection

Spiritual Reality, Science and the Coming King

Sandra A. Micelotti

ISBN 978-1-956010-01-5 (paperback)
ISBN 978-1-956010-02-2 (hardcover)
ISBN 978-1-956010-03-9 (digital)

Copyright © 2021 by Sandra A. Micelotti

All rights reserved. No part of this publication may be reproduced, distributed, or transmitted in any form or by any means, including photocopying, recording, or other electronic or mechanical methods without the prior written permission of the publisher.

Scripture taken from the New King James Version®. Copyright © 1982 by Thomas Nelson. Used by permission. All rights reserved

For permission requests, solicit the publisher via the address and telephone number below.

Rushmore Press LLC 5940 S Rainbow Blvd Las Vegas, NV 89118
1 800 460 9188 www.rushmorepress.com

Printed in the United States of America

Dedication

To my heavenly Father who knew me and loved me before I was in the womb.

When I was a babe, before I could see,
You would appear to comfort me,
When I was a babe, before I could know,
Amazing love for me you did show.

When I was a child, vision unclear
In the night, ridden with fear,
When I was a child, learning to pray,
You visited me; there you would stay.

When I was a girl, oh, so alone,
No understanding, nothing my own,
When I was a girl going astray,
Angels hovered by night and by day.

Now I'm a woman holding you near
With open eyes and ears to hear.
Now I'm a woman, growing in grace,
Until we meet face to face.

Contents

1. Spiritual Reality 1
2. The Godhead 5
3. The Earth and Humanity 11
4. Relationship 15
5. Image and Likeness 18
6. The Preceding Age 22
7. Man's Plummet 28
8. The Ultimate Plan 32
9. The No-No Tree 35
10. Ability and Choice 38
11. Names 41
12. Scientific Conjecture 59
13. The Coming King 66

Conclusion 70

Introduction

Connection is what forms a relationship between any situation and person that affects another; it is crucial in fulfilling purpose and function. High-speed data services interconnect millions of host computers and workstations; human activities interconnect with the environment; people interconnect with people and nations with nations. Whenever a vital connection is lacking, effectiveness and fulfillment are impaired.

Recently, a lovely necklace was given to someone as a gift. After a few weeks of wearing it, the small gold clasp dropped off, and it couldn't be found. Once the clip was missing, the necklace became dismantled. The stones were still beautiful, but they lay on the dresser, powerless, ineffective, unable to be put on display and fulfill the purpose for which they were made. No other type of loop could replace that which became lost; one smaller, larger, or of a different color wouldn't work. Anything aside from the perfect match-made linkage would mar the design and appeal.

Connection is of paramount importance, and there is one to be made that is more vital than all and very key to living a harmonious, thriving existence. However, it cannot be found or formed without giving consideration to spiritual reality and what it entails. Many of us live day-to-day without realizing there exists a realm beyond our physical limits, one from which we have come and to which we belong. In our whirlwind of activity, little thought is given to the matter as we vacillate between believing the subject is mere fantasy, not worth probing or greater than what our faculties can grasp.

In any case, holding this book in your hand indicates that at some level, there is a curiosity churning within you calling to be satisfied. My hope is that in reading this text, you might unearth the link in your life that was disengaged, and make the vital connection. If it has already been discovered and secured, the golden nuggets of truth, beauty, and purpose etched in these pages will magnify the light in which you already walk and add more color to your strand of stones.

1

Spiritual Reality

Many people are wary of spiritual reality. They believe the only reality is what they can see and touch—nothing more. Some go a step further, thinking that there could be an order of things outside the material and physical world. After all, astronauts have traveled to outer space, and there are thousands who insist they have seen flying saucers or had a supernatural experience. Others are absolutely convinced there is another realm beyond the perimeter of this world but have never taken the initiative to acquire knowledge and gain more understanding. Nevertheless, regardless of belief, disbelief, religious persuasion, or lack thereof, the fact remains that we are encompassed by an invisible world full of mysteries waiting to be unmasked.

A vast number of people would agree that human beings are actually spirits housed in bodies designed to accommodate the earth's atmosphere, and that life will continue in some configuration after the body expires. If this is true, the reason for human existence must include something more than being born to live, grow, establish relationships, labor, achieve, reproduce, raise children, and then die. It takes effort and hard work to develop and maintain a productive and fulfilling life. So, living simply to complete the cycle and then forever fade away, or later return to earth in another lower life form such as a cricket is, at best, futile ideology. Therefore, in holding to a view that the spirit of man cannot be extinguished but continues on once the body weakens, breaks down, decomposes, and returns to dust, reason tells us that life *here* has to be in preparation for life *there*.

Now one might ask, "Life there, life where?" This is certainly a fair question but one that can only be answered by peeking in the window of eternity past, then exploring time from its start, and considering eternity future. Varying degrees of detail can be found from three viable sources, two being more restricted than the third. Nature and science provide a good measure of enlightenment but nowhere to the extent of the Bible, which covers at least four thousand years of human history. It was written over a span of approximately fifteen hundred years, from around 1450 BC to about AD 100. More than forty individuals from various professions penned the work.

Of course, there are those who doubt the Bible's validity as well as the existence of God. Nonetheless, the book is historically substantiated work that bears eyewitness accounts. Therefore, referring to it is no different from reading history books or other nonfiction writings, which look back to the distant past. People all over the world have read and continue to read what literature conveys about individuals, places, and events before they were born and, by simple faith, receive the information as authentic.

In regard to the actuality of God, can anyone refute the existence of someone who has never been fully comprehended by the finite mind? Also, throughout the centuries, not a speck of evidence has ever been generated to disprove God's reality but the universe itself declares that he exists. Now with that said, let's shift in reverse and consider some biblical content pertaining to *here* and *there*, starting with an introductory phrase in the very first chapter of the book of Genesis.

2

The Godhead

In the first book of the Bible, the opening phrase, "In the beginning God"[1] announces the commencement of everything and names the orchestrator and conductor. Only one was present at the event—the divine, eternal, independent, self-existent Creator from whom all purpose and action sprang without any outside influence. Given that he was in the beginning, it is reasonable to believe that he was likewise before the beginning. Considering *eternity* and *time* and the distinction between the two will further enhance this understanding.

---

[1] Genesis 1:1

Eternity is perpetual. Prior to the creative acts of God, without any system of measurement in place everything was in eternity, where God dwelled. Time is a period with a limit. It is an extent or a continuation or a length measured by the revolutions of the heavenly bodies. The first day of creation, initiated by space and the structure of matter, marked the inception of time. It stands in the middle of eternity past and eternity future and will continue until this age comes to an end.

Throughout time, the titles "The Godhead" and "God" have been used interchangeably. The former is employed as a synonym of the latter, and denotes the divine essence in distinction from the three persons who are within the Godhead. The name God is translated from the Hebrew word *Elohim,* a plural noun coming from *Eloah.* According to a number of scholars, it is an expanded version of the Semitic singular noun *il.* This word *Elohim,* which is found throughout the first three chapters of Genesis, the first book in the bible, and understood to be grammatically singular, does not imply multiple gods. Instead, it suggests and validates a plurality of persons in the divine nature. In other words, there are three distinct persons in the one Godhead—God the Father, God the Son, and God the Holy Spirit. The verse, "Then God said, let *us* make man in *our* image, according to *our* likeness"[2] helps to crystallize this truth. Also, honorable men of old such as, Isaiah and Paul to name a few, declared with certainty, "The Lord our God is one Lord" "One God and Father of all, who is above all."[3]

During the period of creation, Father God was not working alone but in unison with the two personages within himself. The second person was present in the phrase, "Then God said: 'Let there be light,' and there was light."[4] This utterance was the living Word—God the Son, creatively engaged with the Father, and the Holy Spirit. At a predetermined time in the far

---

[2] Genesis 1:26
[3] Deuteronomy 6:4; Ephesians 4:6
[4] Genesis 1:3

distant future, the Word came to live among men. Owing to the fact that the two are one, the Father was made known through the Son, Jesus, who gave his life for all of humanity in the work of salvation.

Throughout the first portion of Genesis, a relatively short section, "then God said" or "and God said" is spoken a total of nine times. The only begotten Son[5] called into reality the heavens and the earth.

The third person of the Godhead is detected within the expression, "And the Spirit of God hovered over the face of the waters."[6] Here, the Holy Spirit became apparent as he proceeded with the Father and the Son in the development and maturation process of the cosmos. He was poised as would be a mother eagle fluttering over her young or as a nursing hen tending her chicks with great care and affection, nurturing them until they can fly on their own. His

---

[5] John 1:1-5; John 1:14; John 3:16
[6] Genesis 1:2

posture demonstrated the unfathomable love of the triune God for his creation. After the death, resurrection, and ascension of Jesus, God the Holy Spirit was sent to earth to continue revealing to all generations the Father's love through Jesus Christ, and to establish residence within anyone who believes, and is receptive.

So it is that God exists in three co-equal and co-eternal persons. He is not derived from anything or anyone; he is free and autonomous—not created or made. As told in the books of Deuteronomy,[7] Psalms,[8] Isaiah,[9] and The gospel of John,[10] God is essentially and eternally the spirit of never-ending perfection.

Spirit is the highest form of existence and cannot be confined to the restrictions of physical substance. Therefore, although God became man, he is not capable of the limitations of our humanity. He is like no other! He is absolutely

---

[7] Deuteronomy 4:15-16, 19
[8] Psalm 147:5
[9] Isaiah 40:25-26
[10] John 4:24

pure and immeasurably glorious and wondrous; he is superior to any created being. He is without bounds! He not only fills time and space; he transcends time and space. He is so big that descriptions applied to him such as love, light, and fire, and the personal names he has assigned to himself are of unique and sole signification.

3

The Earth and Humanity

It is recorded that on the first day of creation week, God brought into existence the heavens, and the earth.[11] Job, the oldest book of the Bible, tells us that angels, described as "morning stars" and "sons of God," were celebrating the occasion by singing together, worshipping, and shouting for joy.[12] Being as it were, the heavens that came forth refer to the atmosphere around the earth and outer space—the first and second heaven. The third heaven,[13] which occupies God's habitation and throne surrounded by a

---

[11] Genesis 1:1
[12] Job 38:4-7
[13] Corinthians 12:1-4; Revelation 4:2

multitude of angelic beings, emerged at a period unknown before God established the physical universe.

The Earth, central to the creation, is the only hospitable and habitable location for man, and the singular place where all of history occurs. It is unique and distinct from all planets in the solar system, including the other rocky worlds of Mercury, Venus and Mars.

Thick darkness was waiting for the light, the first visible thing spoken into existence.[14] For the initial three days of creation, God was the light. On the second and third days, the sky appeared followed by dry land, grass, herbs, and all fruit-bearing trees. On day four, the Creator fashioned the sun, the moon, and the stars, a part of a wide assortment of celestial bodies. The influence of the Earth's gravitating power was suspended until this fourth day when the sun, around which the earth revolves, was placed in the center.

---

[14] Genesis 1:3-4

The spectacular sun began to deliver daylight and supply energy to warm the earth. The silvery moon received light from the sun and lit up the night. The dazzling stars, which are remote suns, twinkled in the night sky.

God set the lights in place for man's sake, to vivify the natural world, provide luminescence and aesthetic pleasure, serve the earth, and to be used for signs to mark the seasons, days, and years.[15] These symbols of the various changes in the air are vital to agriculture, commerce, and general survival. They are also a visible reminder of the Master's ongoing involvement with, and intense and enduring love for mankind. Had he not called into existence the celestial bodies, this densest planet in the solar system would be nothing more than a wasteland in which neither animal nor vegetable life could be sustained.

Next in the series of related events, man and woman were given rule over all the earth, over the cattle, over everything that creeps and

---

[15] Genesis 1:14-17

crawls, and over the birds of the air and the fish of the sea.[16] This was further affirmation of God's earnest desire to share his world with others.

---

[16] Genesis 1:28

4

Relationship

The Almighty is highly relational! This aspect of his nature becomes easy to perceive in the dawn of time, when everything was brought into existence by the three persons of the Godhead, in collaboration with one another. This distinguishing quality is further established through God's intimate interaction with the first man and woman. It is later reconfirmed when without hesitation he made a way to restore their broken relationship.

The Father, the Son, and the Holy Spirit—one God with a single divine nature—are indivisible, bound together in fellowship that cannot be broken. When creating the universe, they took each other's counsel and worked in unison and harmony. Nevertheless, in spite of this unique bond, God had an unquenchable desire for more family and companionship. He wanted to have others—sons, daughters, and friends, with whom he could walk, talk, and enjoy a relationship. This firm resolve led him to conceive a design for the human race with everything vital for its survival, sustenance, convenience and happiness, eons before the surface of the world or man was formed.

Moving on, the Creator's tenderhearted and amicable character is evidenced in the biblical narration of the Garden of Eden. In the cool of each day, he met with earth's first inhabitants, to simply stroll and chat.[17] In the wee hours of every morning, God of the universe enthusiastically took long walks with Adam and Eve through the beautiful landscape filled with woodland, green pasture, and fragrant flowers. One can only imagine the stimulating, in-depth conversations

---

[17] Genesis 3:8

that transpired, filled with deep tenderness and care, friendship, laughter, ingenuity, and anticipation.

The Creator's motive in making human beings was for nothing less than kinship, and mutual love.[18] That being the case, God never purposed to be mysterious. Long before man became separated from him through disobedience, he devised a concrete method by which men, women, and children of all future generations could acquire reliable knowledge and understanding of his disposition, work, and purpose. Accordingly, the Holy Spirit inspired individuals to write a sizable manual and call it the Bible—a library of sixty-six books, divided into two parts. Imbued with the breath of life, this "book of books" spawns a desire to know more about, and draw closer to the one and only inexhaustible God who loves unconditionally, and is devotedly warm and affectionate.

---

[18] Genesis 1:26

5

Image and Likeness

"Let us make man in our image, after our likeness"[19] addresses the whole person—body, soul, and spirit. The Hebrew word for image, *tselem* means a shadow, an outline of the original, a representative figure. The Hebrew word for likeness, *demuth* means a pattern, resemblance. The two words combined allude to the extrinsic and intrinsic; form and quality.

The use of the terms "us" and "our" versus "me" and "my" further unveils a very important spiritual reality. The words indicate that man is not made in the image and likeness of one or

---

[19] Genesis 1:26.

the other but in the fullness of the Godhead—Father, Son, and Holy Spirit. Therefore, prominently displayed through humans was a full complement of God's inherent characteristics: capacities to love, lead, protect, support, guide, nurture, teach, and comfort.

Mankind was formed after the paragon of God's own nature, to have all of his faculties and to live forever. The human mind was endowed with astounding capabilities, immediately observed through Adam, the first man, who gave a name to every animal. How could he have known what names to assign when he had never before heard them spoken? Like a stream that resembles the spring from which it flows, Adam was endowed with the full mind of God.

Man was not made to be God or hold his position, but he was made to be like him. Although he was formed from the dust of the ground, the breath of life was breathed into his nostrils.[20] The body was shaped from

---

[20] Genesis 2:7

decomposable and perishable material—dirt derived from the earth. However, the spirit, which incorporates the soul, received indestructible life. In this way, in spirit, man was made to be like God and to live eternally. He was patterned to know his Maker, think his thoughts, and have his knowledge fused with wisdom and understanding. He was made to be wise in his mind, holy in his heart, and righteous in his actions.

Another way in which this astonishing being was to resemble his Creator is expressed in God's declaration, "And let them have dominion."[21] Both the man and the woman were delegated governing authority over the entire earth. Possessing time and power, the Sovereign could easily have managed everything himself. Nevertheless, he chose to entrust the task to his loved ones so they could exercise the leadership gift with which they had been

---

[21] Genesis 1:26

endowed, be creative and productive, and enjoy their environment.

After God composed the heavens and earth and made man, he stopped, looked, and said, "Indeed it is very good."[22] This statement intonates the superlative. Everything was not only good; it was as good as it could get; it was perfect. The entire caboodle was a reflection of his being, composed of superior love, goodness, wisdom, power, and beauty.

Man, God's masterpiece of creation, was modeled to be a mirror image of him and his own exceptional features and qualities. He was to know, love, and live with his Maker throughout time-here, and eternity-there, a plan that has never changed.

---

[22] Genesis 1:31

6

The Preceding Age

God framed the worlds and established kingdoms. He created, in heaven and on earth, invisible and visible thrones, dominions, principalities, and powers.[23] The two descriptive nouns, "worlds" and "kingdoms," are indicative of a preceding epoch in which the earliest system of order began. It was in the dateless past, when angels, not men, were granted authority under God to administer his will.

During this earliest Age of Creation, a serious revolt took place that caused a cataclysmic disturbance and brought chaos. Very little detail

---

[23] Hebrews 11:3; Colossians 1:16

can be found pertaining to this episode, but a thumbnail examination of the few facts that are available will bring a broader perspective of the Maker of the Universe and his intentions.

A godly man named Ezekiel wrote about one of the first life forms that the Creator brought into existence.[24] The prophet described the living entity as the most magnificent of anything imaginable, fully arrayed in a jeweled robe, the complete measure of beauty and model of supreme loveliness. This cherub, presented in the imagery of an Asian emperor, was in Eden, the garden of God, and walked on the mountain of God with the makings of percussion and wind instruments built into its being. Another ancient prophet validates Ezekiel's portrayal through his recount of the visible King of Babylon[25]— Nebuchadnezzar II who conquered Jerusalem, juxtaposed with an invisible spiritual king who originally carried the name Lucifer but was later

---

[24] Ezekiel 28:12-14
[25] Isaiah 14:4

given the title Satan and the devil. Isaiah says, "How are you fallen from heaven, O Lucifer, son of the morning! How are you cut down to the ground, which did weaken the nations! For you have said in your heart, I will ascend into heaven, I will exalt my throne above the stars of God: I will sit also upon the mountain of the congregation in the sides of the north: I will ascend above the heights of the clouds; I will be like the Highest. Yet you shall be brought down to hell, to the sides of the pit."[25]

Lucifer, as the Light-Bearer, was covered with nine precious stones to reflect God's glory. He led the worship in heaven and watched over God's throne. He had been granted governmental standing of the highest rank, a position with which he became immensely dissatisfied and grew to despise. Stimulated by greed and lust, he longed to become revered and adored as the sovereign of all creation. He wanted to be surrounded by that assembly of holy

---

[25] Isaiah 14:12

beings gathered for the sole purpose of serving and worshipping the Supreme God. Arrogantly convinced that he, together with his cohorts, could overthrow his originator and take over the kingdoms, he ascended to heaven, north of the earth, and declared war. All of Lucifer's efforts toward exalting himself and becoming like the most High God were instantly thwarted. He and his troops were headed off in their invasion and stopped by the army of God; they were felled as a tree by a woodcutter and utterly defeated. Lucifer, along with the angels that followed his lead, was cast out of God's heaven.

The Creator, equally just as he is loving, compassionate, and full of grace, scrutinized the capability for obedience instilled in the angelic beings. Nobody tempted Lucifer; there was no excuse for his vicious and unremorseful defiance to God's rule. The Light Bearer and his devotees had been in God's presence unceasingly; they knew him and his glory. Still, it didn't stop their relentless jealousy and hostility.

Keeping in line with his remarkable and trustworthy nature, the Creator could not overlook the ensuing exposure. The deliberate transgression against him and his divine law had to be judged in accordance with the amount of knowledge that each possessed. To whom much is given, much is required.[26] Lucifer and the rebellious beings were instantly faced with a verdict of everlasting doom, and all of their previously delegated authority was promptly removed. The conclusion of this sentence will be witnessed at the end of this age when Satan and his emissaries will be cast into the lake of fire, a place of eternal torment.[27]

Lucifer, the earliest one to fall through pride, was responsible for the earth's first sinful history, which brought anarchy into the world and a disorderly state of formlessness and emptiness.[28] Had this being remained true to God, there

---

[26] Luke 12:48
[27] Matthew 25:41, Revelation 20:10
[28] Genesis 1:2

would have been no need to restore the earth to a second livable state with new land, animals, birds, and fish. Lucifer and the pre-Adamites would have continued to exist in God forever, carrying out the marvelous plan designed for them.

7

Man's Plummet

When Adam and Eve disobeyed God, the earth became traumatized, and mankind was faced with unparalleled loss. Satan regained dominion and authority over the kingdoms of the world that would advance, and be filled with people and a system in rebellion against God.[29] Spiritual, physical, and eternal life, the garden home, and daily fellowship with God and the animals were forfeited. Spiritual death was instant; physical death came later in time through sin's degenerative process.

---

[29] John 12:31; Matthew 4:8; Ephesians 2:2

The lifespan of Eve, mother of all the living,[30] is untold, but Adam lived for 930 years,[31] an age almost unimaginable considering the now more common duration to seventy or eighty years.[32]

Once the new rulers of the earth submitted themselves to Satan's deceptive scheme and fell, man's dominion over the planet and his freedom from malevolent behavior became a thing of the past. The course of action they chose brought judgment not only upon them but also upon all who would carry their DNA. Obedience was exchanged for an inferior position, and an appetite to be wicked and act vilely. This led to sickness, pain, sorrow, misery, condemnation, and death. The beauty of holiness was traded for unclean lusts and habits, self-gratification, hardships, sufferings, and other curses too numerous to mention. The beautifully ideal

---

[30] Genesis 3:20
[31] Genesis 5:5
[32] Psalm 90:7-10

nature man was given became mixed with depravity and darkness.

Worst among all loss was communication and friendship with God, plus all the benefits and blessings of being in total union with him. Access to the tree of life, righteousness, complete power to do good, optimal self-control, and perpetual health discontinued.

Since that first offense and injurious fall, idolatry, illness, and disease became rampant, as did theft, murder, molestation, rape, adultery, cruelty, addictions, and physical and emotional abuse. Such tragedies continue to face mankind in one way or another, either directly or indirectly. They are witnessed everywhere, within individual families and/or through relationships with friends, neighbors, and work associates.

Humanity became gravely infected because of the failure to follow one simple instruction. The call to obedience tested man's heart to see if he would, under the most excellent conditions provided, follow his own conscience, remain innocent, accept Father God's love, and be true to him. Although he failed miserably, and the catastrophe caused every descendant of the first man and woman to carry the fallen nature—the inherent propensity to sin, God's love prevailed, evidenced in his next course of action.

8

The Ultimate Plan

Eve allowed herself to be deceived when confronted by the devil and she, along with her husband, sank into a degenerate state. Their eyes began to see things differently. Realizing they were naked, they made themselves a small apron-like garment out of fig leaves.[33] Although this man-made covering was a natural design that served the moment it was totally inadequate to reverse their wrongdoing against God. Only a supernatural pattern, a coat styled by their Maker, could provide recompense and the covering they needed.

---

[33] Genesis 3:7

On the heels of justice came mercy and grace. Without delay, Father God divinely intervened with a demonstration of his recovery plan. He swiftly made tunics of skin with which he clothed the couple,[34] a pivotal act that illustrated something far more significant than attire. This was the greatest pictorial event of all time, masterfully portraying and broadcasting God's strategy for the rescue of man.

In the process of obtaining skins, God had to slay an animal and spill its vital fluid—blood. This was a prophetic act, which promptly showed his deep affection, remarkable grace, and loving kindness toward man. It pointed the way to forgiveness, spiritual reconstruction, and restoration of relationship with the Eternal One for any person with a repentant heart. The maneuver set into motion the astonishing, majestic plan over which the world would one day marvel. It declared three non-negotiable components: salvation could only come from

---

[34] Genesis 3:1

the hand of God, an unblemished, sacrificial, guiltless death substitute had to be offered, and its pure innocent blood had to be shed.

This was preliminary communication concerning the ultimate offering that would be given centuries later for the final reunion between God and man. It pointed to the time when Jesus would willingly give his life for the weak, the ungodly, and the spiritually dead.[35] By the power of the Holy Spirit, God the Son, the second person of the Godhead, would come to earth, be born of a woman, and become the living innocent sacrifice that would be given once, for humanity.

---

[35] Romans 5:8

9

The No-No Tree

God formed man, breathed into him, and then gave him life-sustaining instruction. He told Adam that he could enjoy eating the yield of every woody plant in the garden, except for the tree of the knowledge of good and evil. He was forewarned that he would die if he consumed the forbidden fruit,[36] a caution he would later share with his wife, Eve.

For many, this incident has given rise to the following question, "If God so loved all that he created, and there is truly no evil in him, why would he have intentionally situated something

---

[36] Genesis 2:17

in the midst of the garden that could lead to man's demise?" Well, except for sampling the fruit, the stately and inviting tree with all of its produce was absolutely harmless. It stood merely to serve as a witness that Adam and Eve had complete liberty to choose their course of action and make decisions for themselves. The culprit that paved the way for death's entry was not the "No-No Tree," it was their deliberate and willful disobedience.

The Master's greatest aspiration was for his companions to obey and live forever, both physically and spiritually. Nonetheless, they were not pre-programmed or coerced into following the Father's counsel. He gave them an independent will to exercise in making choices moment-to-moment, and day-to-day. Deciding to act contrary to his leading displayed disrespect and a lack of confidence in his love, goodness, and protection for their lives. In not following the direction given for their benefit, and insisting on satisfying their own curiosity, they instantly removed themselves from the one who had been to them both Father and friend.

Whenever God is ignored or rejected, and his counsel is dismissed wrongdoing will surely arise and show its ugly head. After *the vital connection* was broken, Adam and Eve could no longer operate in the Master's "likeness." The *spirit* within them became dark and functionally dead; *soul power* (mind, will, and emotion) was insufficient to keep them walking in divine enlightenment. Embracing one lie after another, they were deceived into believing that their strength and mental abilities were more than enough, and they had little need for God.

The eyes of Adam and Eve were opened to evil. Strange new impressions triggered thoughts, which had never before entered their imagination. Finally, unable to stand in the light of a pure, holy, and righteous God, shame led them to run and hide from the lover of their souls.

10

Ability and Choice

Some have voiced, "If there is one Sovereign who knows all things and is unerring, how could he have made such massive blunders? How could there have been such imperfection in his creation? Firstly, he formed a being, which rebelled against him, became his archenemy, and induced others accordingly. Secondly, he produced human beings who disrespected him, ignored him, and sinned against him. If truly infallible and omniscient, in his foreknowledge, wouldn't the Creator have prevented this from happening?"

It is impossible for God, who has an intrinsic nature that is flawless and faultless, to have erred or to ever make a mistake. The heavenly beings and man, shaped in the integrity of God, fully mature, intelligent, and without a blemish, had a favorable onset. They were bestowed with every quality and characteristic necessary to live forever in blissful harmony and fellowship with God Supreme. However, not formed as a puppet to be manipulated at the will of another, not even that of their Maker, they were given the ability to choose, wisely or unwisely.

Ability, the quality that facilitates achievement, is not an imperfect attribute; it simply provides the capacity to decide one-way or another. The ability to do wrong and doing wrong are not synonymous, and capacity does not equate to incompleteness or faultiness. For these reasons, the angelic rebellion of heaven and man's disobedience are not indications of anything having been defective. The ultimate shift to sinful imperfection from the original state of sinless perfection was wholly the result of willful choice.

More often than not, leaders who are insecure, feel threatened or grow fearful of losing control become dictators. However, the one and only God of the Universe does not fall into this category. Worry, anxiety, fear, unease, insecurity, and uncertainty cannot find a place in him or in any statement he has made or action he has taken. Possessing complete knowledge, wisdom, and power, the Almighty has everything required to correct and accomplish whatever would be necessary if or when things go awry. He is more than competent to heal and restore as well as to create and redeem.

So it was that in spite of having been entirely aware of the consequences that could arise from prideful disobedience in his plan of creation, God opted not to eliminate from the angelic beings or from man, the ability to choose. He readily allowed the character traits of trust and loyalty toward him—the foundation of pure love, to be tested.

11

Names

In the ancient world, personal names were viewed a little differently than in contemporary society. Today, our given name or the one by which we refer to ourselves, is used for casual and intimate identification and personal greeting. However, in very early history, names took on far more meaning. Knowing an individual's name and addressing the person accordingly was considered a unique privilege that offered access to his or her thoughts and life.

God was the first to exemplify this concept. Every time he personally assigned names to people and places, directly or indirectly, they carried meaning and provided insight into the essence of the individuals or the sites that were being earmarked. Furthermore, our Creator understood the importance of providing man with descriptive titles by which he could be addressed and through which something significant about him could be discovered. This simple, uncomplicated, straightforward method has enabled humankind to become acquainted with his personal characteristics and distinguishing attributes.

Over one hundred biblical names for God can be cited. Following are samplings that relate the radiance of his impeccable nature and render special insight into his reality, personality, love, and righteousness.

El is one of the oldest words for God to be found in the Hebrew language. It is a root word meaning "strength," "power," "might," and "prominent." Traditionally, it expresses the idea of a singular deity but is typically qualified by linking on additional words to expand its definition and unfold a wealth of knowledge. Following are significant examples.

Elohim, a name by which God referred to himself in the first chapter of the Bible,[37] and one used innumerably within the Old Testament, was touched upon earlier in the text. Attention was given to the fact that this proper noun is plural but when used in reference to the one and only Creator of the cosmos and the human race, the word refers to the fullness of the Godhead, never to multiple gods.

Although concealed from the human eye for centuries, this appellation strongly proclaimed the invaluable and unprecedented rescue plan of God and declared his good, compassionate, and forgiving nature. Before man existed and his need for salvation became apparent, the blueprint for his recovery was devised. The three persons of the Godhead discussed and agreed that the second person, the Son, would become flesh, go to the Cross-, take upon himself every sin of humanity, give his blood as an offering,

---

[37] Genesis 1:26

and open heaven's gates to mankind. They concurred he would be named Jesus.

This caption bore witness to God's unquenchable love and desire to have mankind with him long before man was formed. It spoke loudly of the Lord's omniscience and his redemptive power.

El Elyon means "God Most High" or "the Most Exalted God." The initial use of this label is found in the first chapter of the Bible, where it is repeated four times.[38] Here the Lord is typified through the appearance of one called Melchizedek, King of Salem and priest of God Most High. Melchizedek is an ancient Canaanite name meaning "My King is Righteousness." He approached a man called Abraham, pronounced a blessing over him, and made clear that he had been his source of victory in battle.

The illustration served to show the Creator as the initiator of relationships, caring and involving himself in the lives of all who love

---

[38] Genesis 14:18-22

him, demonstrating his power on their behalf. Additionally, it was a prophetic portrayal of Jesus, Son of God, Prince of Peace, Great High Priest, and The Righteousness of man.[39]

The title El Elyon endorses God's perfection, exalted nature, sovereignty, and dominion; it asserts that he is the only one to be worshiped. It is used throughout the first covenant of the Bible twenty-eight times and always when God was personally involved in blessing his people with either divine revelation of himself, deliverance from an enemy, or healing.

El Shaddai is a name for God that signifies "Almighty God" and "Strength-Giver," "Satisfier," and the "All-Sufficient One" who enriches. When a man called Abraham was ninety-one years old, God appeared to him. He spoke with him, encouraged him to continue walking with him in obedience, and blessed him superabundantly. He vowed that his favor would be upon him, his descendants would be

---

[39] Luke 1:32; Isaiah 9:6; Hebrews 7:26-28; Philippians 3:9

many and they would constitute a nation. God declared that all people on the earth would be blessed through Abraham.

In so presenting himself, God was making a statement that in him, with him, and through him nothing is impossible. As the Almighty,[40] he is thoroughly capable and willing to do any good thing for those who believe in him and love him.

Through the tag El Shaddai, God is illuminated as the "Omnipotent" with none to compare. He is the root of blessing for mankind and the entire universe. He is colossal with everything under his control and serving his purpose.

Jehovah, the name proclaimed by God in revealing himself to ancient Israel, is sometimes transcribed *Yahweh*. The two are used interchangeably because the name originates from the Hebrew verb "to be," which is spelled *YHWH* and translated "I Am Who I Am." This

---

[40] Genesis 17:1-2, 35:11

word is all encompassing and incorporates the expression, "I will be who I will be." It was first used when God revealed himself to Moses at a burning bush and said, "Tell the people, 'I Am has sent me to you.'"[41] The setting itself is a vivid symbol of the inexhaustible dynamism of God who burns like fire, with love, righteousness, and goodness.

The title speaks of constancy, affirming that God is the same forever and faithful to fulfill all of his promises. In this world of continual change, where nothing and nobody can be found unfailing, the "Strength-Giver" who is absolutely immutable says what he means, and means what he says.

The name further states that God is the all-powerful and sovereign. Nobody can define who he is but himself. Nature and the Bible stand together on this planet as an infallible guide to knowing him. "I Am" proclaims that the infinite and original personal God is behind the

---
[41] Exodus 3:14-15

whole ball of wax and the one to whom everyone will give account at the end of time. He alone established truth and the way of salvation; facts made blatantly apparent by the next seven name combinations starting with "Jehovah." These captions purposefully revealed his redemptive attitude toward humanity.

Jehovah-Shammah, "The Lord is there" or "The Lord is present" was the name heard by the prophet Ezekiel in a vision. Foresight was given to him of God's promise for the future rebuilding of the temple. He was told that Israel would be restored from the Babylonian captivity, which happened at the height of her idolatry and rebellion, and that the reconstruction would begin when he brought the people back to Jerusalem.

The title pointed to both the near and distant future, when God's divine presence would be so powerful in the city of Jerusalem that its name would be changed to Jehovah-

Shammah,[42] and the period when Jesus, Son of God, Savior of man, would make Israel his residence. It also foretold about the church, the people of God becoming his temple—the place in which the Holy Spirit would reside, and of the New Jerusalem, God's eternal dwelling place.

The Lord is not only *here*, with us today for every situation of our lives waiting to be called upon, but he is already *there* in our tomorrows. Anyone distant from God can become close through the blood of Christ.[43] He is ready, willing, and able to help in times of trouble.[44]

Jehovah-Shalom, "the Lord Our Peace," was a name assigned to an altar built by a gentleman called Gideon,[45] who grieved over the oppression and suffering of his people. Although of no particular repute, God viewed him as a mighty man of valor. He entrusted him with a commission beyond his natural ability,

---

[42] Ezekiel 48:35
[43] Ephesians 2:13
[44] Psalm 46:1
[45] Judges 6:24

and then comforted, encouraged, and assured him of victory. In commemoration of having received great favor and peace with God along with a promise of miraculous success in the battle against Israel's enemies, Gideon erected a memorial.

Throughout history, at one time or another and for various reasons, hostility has existed between nations as well as individuals on a personal level. This ongoing condition that abounds from shore to shore is one for which ways and means of peace are constantly being pursued. Yet, the greatest peace to be obtained is that to which the name Jehovah-Shalom alludes—lasting peace with the Father. The only road to this peace is through faith in Jesus the Christ and his redemptive love.[46]

Jehovah-Raah or *Jehovah-Rohi,* translated "The Lord is My Shepherd," is a title by which Jacob and King David, both leaders of

---

[46] Romans 5:1

Israel in ancient times, addressed God.[47] Their own history in pastoral life enabled them to understand the perspective of sacrificial love embedded in this name. Nobody knew better than these men that a good shepherd would lay down his life to protect his herd from ravenous wolves.[48] Use of the name expressed personal praise to the Lord, and acknowledgment that he is always providing for the needs of his people and giving special consideration to the young and weak.

This term Jehovah-Raah depicts a loving herdsman guiding his sheep. Likewise, Jesus leads all those who follow him by faith out of the dry, sparse fields, and muddy water into flourishing green pastures with pure, clean springs. In the scorching heat of life, he provides shade and watchful protection.

Jehovah Nissi, "The Lord Our Victor" or "the Lord Our Banner," is the name of an altar

---

[47] Genesis 49:24; Psalm 23:1; Psalm 80:1
[48] John 10:11

of commemoration built by Moses, the man God chose to deliver Israel from the bondage of Egypt.[49] Shortly after he began leading the people through the wilderness, he encountered their first enemy, Amalek. Seeing the opposition, Moses instructed his assistant Joshua to form a military squad and enter into combat against the Amalekites. At the same time, he proceeded up the sloping trail with his brother Aaron and companion, Hur who came from the tribe of Judah—a word meaning "praise." Upon reaching the peak of the hill, Moses stood with his staff in his hands, and raised them toward heaven. As long as they remained lifted, the soldiers were victorious but when they dropped from weariness, the Amalekites prevailed. So, Aaron and Hur positioned themselves on each side of Moses, holding up his arms until sunset when the battle was won.

Prayer and praise were extended through Moses while Joshua was confronting the

---

[49] Exodus 17:15

enemy. The staff of Moses on display like a flag represented the everlasting Kingdom of God and its King, who is more powerful than a sword. This posture encouraged the troops and reminded them of guaranteed victory because they were fighting by the Lord's direction, and under his banner. The battle typified Christ's triumphant death on the Cross and his conquest of all spiritual principalities and powers, a wonder that would occur more than a millennium later.[50]

As delineated by the name Jehovah Nissi, in and through Jesus the Christ, the enemy of man's soul is defeated. Just as Joshua stood for the Israelites and Moses interceded, Jesus always stands on behalf of those who embrace him and intervenes in the affairs of their lives.

Jehovah-Jireh announces "The Lord Will Provide."[51] This recalls a specific time when God greatly provided for Abraham, a man he asserted

---

[50] Colossians 2:15
[51] Genesis 22:14

to be his friend.[52] Training and building his faith, God asked him to take his only son, go to the land of Moriah, construct an altar of wood, and offer Isaac as a sacrifice.[53] Focusing on his relationship with the Creator and believing in his love and goodness rather than on how the situation appeared, Abraham humbly walked in faith and trust, and followed instructions. He was not disappointed. At the precise moment of need a male sheep appeared from out of the bushes. God told Abraham to pick up the ram and place it on the altar of sacrifice in lieu of Isaac.

Evidenced in the name Jehovah-Jireh and in the account above was a portrayal of what would occur in the distant future when God would send his only Son to earth and allow him to be sacrificed for the sin of the human race. God's love is loyal and unequaled.

---

[52] Isaiah 41:8; 2 Chronicles 20:7; James 2:23
[53] Genesis 22:2-3

Jehovah-Tsidkenu, "The Lord Our Righteousness" is a name for God that was utilized twice by Jeremiah, an Old Testament prophet who was charged with delivering a sobering message to Judah. He informed the nation and its people of impending consequences if they continued in idolatry and rebellion.[54] Multiple forewarnings were given as a display of God's justice tempered with mercy, and in an effort to elicit desire within the nation to change direction and avoid imminent misfortune.

This name Jehovah-Tsidkenu prefigured two faraway events. The first was the time when Jesus would become the justification in which anyone receiving his sacrifice on the Cross could stand for a renewed relationship with the Father. The second was his return as King to establish his earthly rule, reign in wisdom and righteousness,[55] and be recognized by the nation

---
[54] Jeremiah 23:6, 33:16
[55] Revelation 11:15

of Israel as the true Messiah[56]—a sure happening yet to occur!

Jehovah-Rapha means "I am the Lord who heals" or personally expressed, "I am your physician."[57] After more than two million Israelites had been miraculously delivered out of the bondage of slavery in Egypt and brought through the Red Sea, they were taken by Moses into the wilderness of Shur, presently known as Saudi Arabia. They traveled three days without drinking until they came to a place called Marah where water was plentiful but unfit for consumption. Noting the utter dismay of the people, Moses immediately cried out to the Lord for help. He was directed to a tree and instructed to throw it into the water. Instantly, and to everyone's delight, the previously bitter taste became sweet.

According to the biblical perspective, wood is often used as a symbol of man. It also brings

---

[56] Romans 11:6
[57] Exodus 15:26

to mind the cross, made of two wooden planks nailed together. Bearing on this understanding, an analogy can be seen between the tree that was cast into the water in the Arabian Desert and the voice of God crying out in man's wilderness, narrating his grace, love, and mercy toward humanity. The phenomenon at Marah presented a preview of the divine plan to liberate man from the bitterness of sin.

The title Jehovah-Rapha affirmed that God is the one and only cure for the illness that brought about spiritual death and eventually caused debilitating ramifications in the body and soul of man. No physician is able to heal other than Jesus who carried upon himself all of the sin and guilt, sickness and disease of mankind.[58]

Jesus means "Yahweh saves," "Yahweh is Salvation" or "The Lord is salvation." Transliterated from Hebrew and Aramaic the name is Yeshua, which in English is spelled Joshua. However, when the name Yeshua is

---

[58] Isaiah 53:4-5; Psalm 103:2-4; Matthew 8:17

translated from Hebrew into Greek, it becomes Iēsous, which in English becomes Jesus.

The name of Jesus is above all names. It is highest name of God ever revealed and the most extraordinary, powerful, and supreme revelation of God. It proclaims his greatest work among humanity, unveils his divine nature to the world, and bears the fullest expression of the redemptive descriptions and disclosures previously delineated. The name Jesus embodies the fullness of God's glory. Salvation can be found in no person other than Jesus, and forgiveness can only be received through his name.[59]

---

[59] Acts 4:12; Acts 10:43

12

Scientific Conjecture

A number of history books used today in high schools and colleges allege that due to an aggregation of matter throughout the centuries and a series of natural developments, the world and man materialized by way of either chance or universal law. For instance, the "Big Bang Theory," derived from mathematical formulas, is considered to be one of the leading explanations of how the universe originated. It states that billions of years ago, everything emerged suddenly, in a single moment of time. "Evolution" is another hypothesis that is deemed to be among the most scientifically proven, and asserts that all different species evolved from simple life forms. This particular conjecture has been a matter of serious discourse, and ranks very high in popularity. So, it is worthy of examination to see how it weighs against the sole record of creation left to man.

Evolution assumes the human being to be offspring of the ape together with a long series of vertebrates; that is, animals with a backbone or spinal column. However, it is necessary to understand some significant facts regarding this supposition. There is no undeniable proof to substantiate that the human being was originally protoplasm, which gradually evolved into an ape, and then mysteriously developed into a man. In addition, evolutionists boldly declare that no sharp boundary line, in physical, mental, or moral structure, has ever been found between man and that from which he presumably sprang. Even for those who hold fast to the theory of evolution, completely bridging the gap between the ape and man has been an insoluble dilemma.

Apes have been taught and have learned how to communicate with human beings at some level, and dolphins do have a brain almost as large as that of a man. However, there is not a single statistic nor a shred of evidence to support that either of these mammals have stepped beyond a very low level of tutoring in learning or have anywhere near the capacity of man for higher education. Nobody has ever seen an ape or a dolphin sitting in a primary school, middle school, high school, college classroom, or training to work with electronics or fashion design. Neither mammal has equaled or substituted the performance of a man. If teaching them everything that a human being knows and comprehends was possible, it would certainly have been done by now, if for no other reason than to prove the point.

A remark once made by Plato and the comment he received from a peer, paints a rather suitable picture for this subject. He defined man as a "two-legged animal without feathers." Diogenes, another ancient Greek philosopher, mocked him for having made such a ridiculous statement. To demonstrate the absurdity,

Diogenes produced a plucked rooster, held it up, and said, "This is Plato's man."[60]

Scientists say they have proven dolphins can learn how to speak, but what languages have they spoken, and with whom have they conversed beside themselves in their own way? Documentation verifies that much of a dolphin's brain is taken up with locating objects by reflected sound and handling acoustical information, processes at which they very much excel. It is also proven that they communicate with one another and are exceptional at mimicking noise and tone, including vowel sounds. Nonetheless, they remain void of factual language skills and are unable to mimic a consonant, a very basic sound of human speech.

One of the most marked distinctions between man and beast is the gift of expressing thought in an articulate speech. Certain animals and birds, such as parrots and parakeets, are famous for imitating the human voice and

---

[60] Diogenes, Book 6: *The Cynics*

uttering a few words but nothing more. Language requires a peculiar intelligence, which has been apportioned to man alone. Every living thing on earth may communicate at some base level, but only human beings have been granted the gift of language. Unlike an ape or a dolphin, man possesses the power of speech and can transcribe thoughts. A vast assortment of literature covering a multitude of topics, including poetry and the highest movements of music have been written, and also translated, by men and women in every vernacular.

The size of the human brain is out of proportion to the mental needs of the highest animal below man. Extensive research reports that the weight of the largest brain of a gorilla is far less than half of the average person and only one-third of the most developed brain of the human race. So, an impassable gulf of reasoning power separates man from lower creation because his intellectual capacity belongs to a completely different order.

Man's remarkable faculty of reasoning, along with his power to acquire knowledge and ability to reach conclusions for practical results and application, goes unsurpassed. Inferior creatures stand dumb when it comes to the diverse issues and predicaments of life. They have instinct, but only man has the intellect to guide him in decision-making and developing. George Romanes, an eminent scientist from Oxford who lived during the mid- to late 1800s, collected the demonstration of intelligent reasoning of every known species of the lower animals. He discovered that all combined equaled the intelligence of a fifteen-month-old child.

Man is the sole figure in God's creation with a moral quality to discerning the difference between good and bad, right and wrong, and with a desire to worship. At the moment God's breath was breathed into man, he received a consciousness of him, along with an absolute knowing that he exists. This is the reason why throughout history and among all people groups, biblical declarations about God have elicited praise, worship, adoration, and love toward him.

Some people adhere to notions that deny God made man, but could an infant so intricately designed and finely tuned just happen? The human being has faculties no other creature possesses. He is able to imagine, think, and comprehend. Among all life on earth, only man has the capacity to see God in all of his work, recognize his infinite wisdom, appreciate his goodness, and marvel at his power. John Milton, the blind poet, could perceive this truth clearly as he wrote: "All these his wondrous works, but chiefly man."[61]

Everything has been made after its own kind,[62] so man and animals are without a common origin. Mankind was created in the Divine image and likeness, an identification of supreme honor.

---

[61] Book 3 of Paradise Lost
[62] Genesis 1:24-25

13

The Coming King

Jesus, the Son of God, was born of a woman and walked on this earth over two thousand years ago. The Word who became flesh and dwelt among us, spoke the world into existence, created man from the dust of the ground, and breathed life into him. Then, he came to this planet to reveal the Father's love and character and let everyone know that he is warm, friendly, and approachable.

At the age of thirty-three, Jesus was nailed to a tree, shed his precious blood, and died to satisfy the law's holy demand for a perfect sacrifice without spot or blemish. He willingly gave his life, and took upon himself the sin of humanity so that every man, woman and child could have the opportunity to be restored into a right relationship with the Father and enjoy companionship with him forever. Jesus rose from the grave victor over sin and death; he ascended into heaven to sit at the right hand of the Father, and to send the Holy Spirit to earth. Jesus opened the gates of heaven for anyone who desires to know him, and is willing to acknowledge personal sin, and ask for forgiveness.

The drama has not yet ended; the world stage is being prepared for the final act. Jesus is returning to planet earth but this time as King, an upcoming event, which is breathtaking and immeasurable in its implications. The human mind cannot fully fathom the incalculable and eternal impact this will have on the entire universe. The second person of the Godhead will be seen coming with clouds, great power, and glory. His elect will be gathered together from the four winds; that is, from the farthest part of earth to the farthest part of heaven.[63] Every knee will bow before Jesus and all of humanity will recognize him according to the title he has been given: "King of kings and Lord of lords."[64] The world will be transformed, justice will be administered, transgressors will be judged, and faithfulness will be rewarded.

Christ's return will be the marvel of human history and a time when righteousness will be established in the earth. Everyone and everything in the universe will be brought into his all-powerful and compelling supremacy. The heavens and the earth, the righteous and the unrighteous, angels and demons, life and death, time and eternity will come under the dominion of the conquering King. Therefore, it is a lack of wisdom to associate indifference, as many do, to the now opulent display of God's wonderful attribute of long-suffering as he waits for humanity to receive his love and saving grace.

---

[63] Matthew 13:26–27
[64] Revelation 17:14, 19:16

Jesus said, "For as the lightning comes out of the east and shines even unto the west; so, shall also the coming of the Son of man be."[65] Jesus—Son of God, Son of man, Messiah, the Son of the living God, the Word made flesh, the Christ, the finished work of Christ, Lord, Lamb of God, Savior of the World, God himself, is soon to return as King of kings and Lord of lords.

---

[65] Matthew 24:27

Conclusion

The Creator of the universe made ample provision for mankind from eternity past; he conceived within himself a detailed diagram of how obedience would be exchanged for disobedience and life for death. Then he displayed a prototype in ancient Israel for centuries, over fifty generations, until the plan was put into the womb of a teenager called Mary and became visible through the birth of Jesus who is both completely God and completely man. The divine strategy was presented to generation upon generation through innumerable names, prophetic words, illustrations, and exemplification so that nobody would forget, become hopeless, or think God had forgotten them. Although the plan is no longer obscure, God continues to broadcast this spiritual reality, desiring that none miss out on making *The Vital Connection*.

www.ingramcontent.com/pod-product-compliance
Lightning Source LLC
Chambersburg PA
CBHW021450070526
44577CB00002B/346